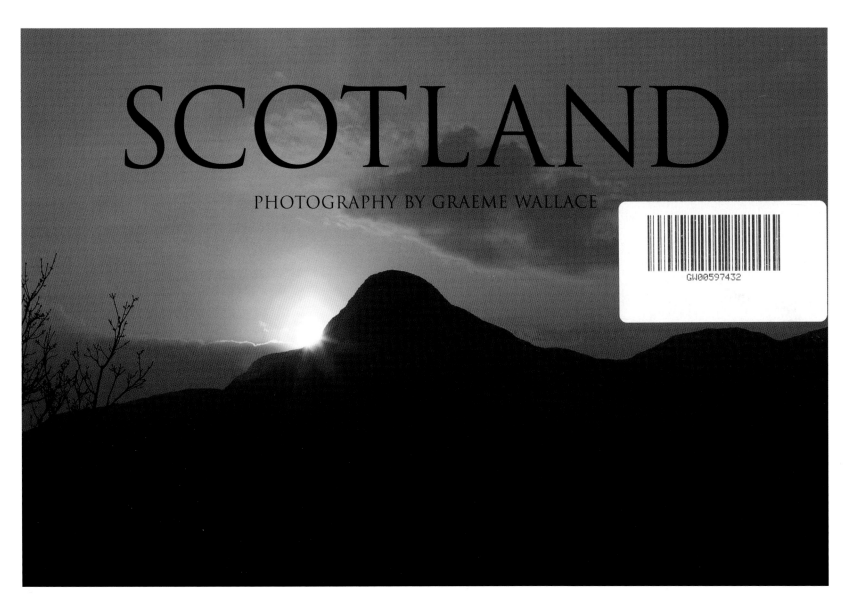

SCOTLAND

PHOTOGRAPHY BY GRAEME WALLACE

Paps of Glencoe (741m) at sunrise, near Ballachulish, Highland

Old pack-horse bridge, Carrbridge, Inverness-shire, Highland

Scotland is a country renowned for the beauty and range of its landscapes, from forbidding and spectacular mountains to rolling and cultivated farmland, from cliffs three-hundred metres high to long white sandy beaches, from ancient and remote Caledonian forest to busy but beautiful cities, not least Edinburgh, Scotland's capital.

Scotland can be divided into three rough geographic areas, shaped by geological events over millions of years. The south of Scotland is known for its rolling hills and valleys and fertile farmland; the central lowlands, flatter and lower and more industrialised, is where most of the population now live; while the Highlands are renowned for the magnificent mountains and deep glens and island-studded seas.

The Highlands have some of Scotland's most spectacular scenery, as well as interesting wildlife on land and sea: Highland cattle, deer, red squirrels, golden eagles, ospreys, multitudes of seabirds, whales, dolphins and porpoises – and even wallabies on an island in Loch Lomond. Haunting Ben Nevis, rising to 1343 metres, is the highest mountain in the British Isles, and the Cairngorms are an impressive mountain range, with several peaks over 1000 metres high. Picturesque Loch Ness is reputed to be the home
of Nessie or the Loch Ness Monster, while Glencoe, also known as the Vale of Tears and one of the most atmospheric places to be found anywhere in the world, is the scene of the famous massacre in 1692.

The population of Scotland is around five million people, and many Scots live in the major cities of Edinburgh and Glasgow in the central belt, and Aberdeen in the north-east. Edinburgh has long been Scotland's capital. It is dominated by the massive castle perched on its volcanic rock above the town and the extinct volcano Arthur's Seat, making Edinburgh one of the most beautiful cities in Europe. The centre of the city is divided into the Old and New Towns. The Old Town, a warren of tenements and closes, was built down the Royal Mile to the Palace of Holyroodhouse, the palace of the monarchs of Scotland and now the Queen's official residence in Scotland. The New Town is a Georgian masterpiece of planned streets and crescents and gardens. One of the many highlights of the city is the excellent Museum of Scotland, which features artefacts from the earliest times to the present day.

Glasgow was a powerhouse of the British Empire during the industrial revolution, and was a hub of shipbuilding, trade and commerce. The old part of the city is centred on the beautiful medieval cathedral, the only one on mainland Scotland to have survived the Reformation intact. The city has many attractions, not least the excellent range of shops, and superb museums and galleries such as the Burrell Collection, the newly restored Kelvingrove Museum and St Mungo's Museum of Religious Life and Art. St Mungo is Glasgow's patron saint, and it is to him that the cathedral is also dedicated.

Aberdeen, also known as the Granite City because so many of the buildings are constructed from grey granite, is built around two rivers, the Don and the Dee. Its ancient heart, Old Aberdeen, was further north than the present centre, and was built around St Machar's Cathedral and the University of Aberdeen. The university was founded at the end of the fifteenth century, and incorporates the beautiful King's College, which has an unusual crown spire. In more recent times the city has become associated with the oil industry and exploration in the North Sea.

The Western Isles or Hebrides, off the west coast of the country, are a beautiful group of islands, and are as different from each another as from any other part of Scotland. Some are mountainous, such the Isle of Skye with the jagged saw-tooth Cuillin hills; others are low and flat but with beautiful sandy beaches and colourful wildflowers in the late Spring. The Western Isles have a distinct Gaelic culture, and many of the inhabitants speak Gaelic, an ancient tongue once spoken throughout much of Scotland.

The many islands of Orkney and Shetland lie off the north coast of Scotland, and are located in some of the roughest seas in the world. There are many Viking influences, and the islands did not become part of Scotland until the middle of the fifteenth century. Orkney has some of the best prehistoric monuments in the whole of Europe, and the islands are beautiful and atmospheric.
The famous rock stack called the Old Man of Hoy and the high cliffs of St John's Head on the Isle of Hoy are especially impressive.

Shetland is lower and less fertile than Orkney. It is in the islands' capital, Lerwick, that the famous Up Helly Aa celebrations, a Viking-inspired festival which features the burning of a Norse longboat, are held every January.

SCOTLANDS REGIONS

SHETLAND

ORKNEY

OUTER HEBRIDES

HIGHLANDS & SKYE

ABERDEEN & GRAMPIAN

ANGUS & DUNDEE

PERTHSHIRE

ARGYLL, THE ISLES, LOCH LOMOND,
STIRLING & THE TROSSACHS

KINGDOM OF FIFE

EDINBURGH & THE LOTHIANS

GREATER GLASGOW & CLYDE VALLEY

AYRSHIRE & ARRAN

DUMFRIES & GALLOWAY

SCOTTISH BORDERS

CONTENTS

Caerlaverock Castle, near Dumfries, Dumfries and Galloway

Dunure Bay, Ayr looking across the Firth of Clyde to the Isle of Arran

Orchardton Tower, near Dalbeattie, Kirkcudbrightshire, Dumfries and Galloway – *opposite*

Burns Cottage, Alloway, near Ayr, Ayrshire

Culzean Castle, near Maybole, Ayrshire

Looking down on the Royal Burgh of Peebles, Scottish Borders

Bass Rock, near North Berwick,
East Lothian

Stable block at Crichton Castle,
near Gorebridge, Midlothian –
opposite

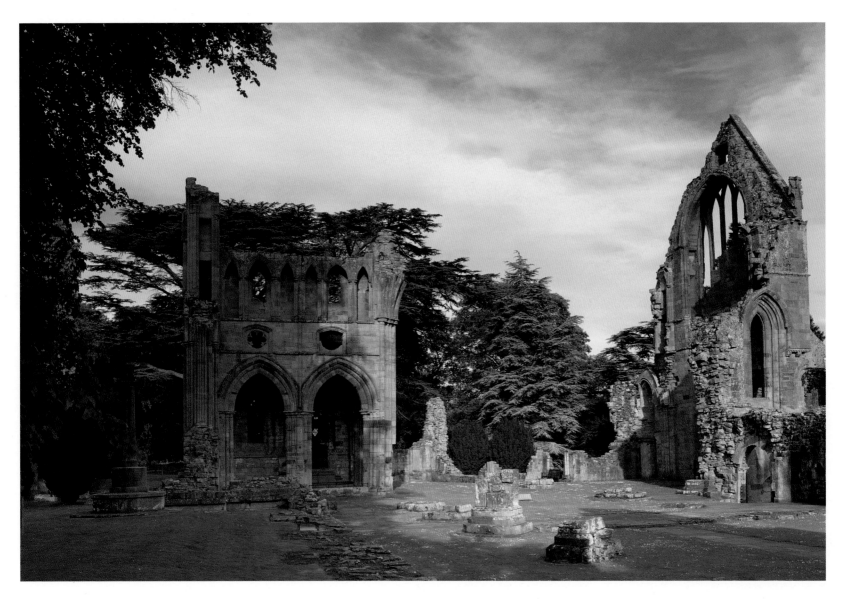

Dryburgh Abbey, near Melrose, Roxburghshire, Scottish Borders

Scott's View to the Eildon Hills, near Melrose, Roxburghshire, Scottish Borders

St Mungo's Museum of Religion Life and Art, Glasgow

New Lanark village, near
Lanark, South Lanarkshire

Glasgow Cathedral, Glasgow

City Chambers, George Square, Glasgow – *opposite*

Edinburgh from Arthur's Seat

Camera Obscura and the
Tolbooth Church, Castlehill,
Royal Mile, Edinburgh

West Bow and Victoria Street, Edinburgh

Edinburgh Castle, Edinburgh – *opposite*

Blackness Castle, near Linlithgow, West Lothian

Linlithgow Palace, Linlithgow, West Lothian

Falkirk Wheel, Falkirk

Fintry Hills (482m), Stirlingshire – *opposite*

ROBERT
THE
BRUCE
KING
OF
SCOTS
1306-1329

Robert the Bruce Statue,
Bannockburn Heritage Centre, Stirlingshire

Stirling Castle, Stirling

National Wallace Monument, Abbey Craig, Stirlingshire

Loch Lomond from Gartocharn, Dunbartonshire – *opposite*

Loch Achray and Ben Venue
(729m), near Aberfoyle,
Trossachs, Stirlingshire

SS Sir Walter Scott, Trossachs pier, Loch Katrine, Stirlingshire

Isle of Mull ferry, Oban harbour, Argyll

Tarbert, Kintyre, Argyll – *opposite*

Tobermory, Isle of Mull, Argyll

Ardmucknish Bay and Benderloch, Argyll – *opposite*

Falls of Dochart, Killin, Perthshire

Castle Stalker with the Kingairloch Mountains in distance, Loch Linnhe, Appin, Argyll – *opposite*

PERTHSHIRE, ANGUS & DUNDEE
and KINGDOM OF FIFE

Fertile Farmland, near Douglastown, Forfar, Angus

Blair Castle, Blair Atholl, Perthshire – *opposite*

Highland Cow

Loch Tummel and Schiehallion (1081m) from Queen's View, near Pitlochry, Perthshire – *opposite*

Hay bails, near Loch Leven, Kinross

St Andrews Cathedral, St Andrews, Fife

Upper Largo, Fife

Glamis Castle, Glamis, Angus – *opposite*

Aberdeen City Skyline including the Town House clock tower

King's College, Old Aberdeen

Dunnottar Castle, near Stonehaven, Kincardineshire – *opposite*

Balmoral Castle, near Ballater, Royal Deeside, Aberdeenshire

River Spey, near Grantown-on-Spey, Strathspey, Highland

Pennan, Aberdeenshire

Elgin Cathedral, Elgin, Moray

Deer Stag – *opposite*

Cairngorm Mountains with Ben Nevis in far distance, Highland

Loch Morlich and the Cairngorm Mountains, near Aviemore, Strathspey, Highland

Bidean nam Bian (1148m),
Glen Coe, near Ballachulish,
Highland – *opposite*

Clan MacDonald Monument,
Glencoe, Highland

Corran Ferry, Loch Linnhe, to Sgurr Dhomhnuill (888m), near Fort William, Highland   Loch Eilt and Rois-Bheinn (877m), near Glenfinnan, Moidart, Highland – *opposite*

Loch Linnhe and Creach Bheinn (853m), Argyll – *opposite*

Loch Ness from Fort Augustus, Inverness-shire, Highland

Isle of Skye Bridge, Kyle of Lochalsh, Highland

Eilean Donan Castle, Loch Alsh, across to Sgurr na Coinnich (732m) on the Isle of Skye, Highland – *opposite*

Beinn na Caillich (732m), near Broadford, Isle of Skye, Highland

Cuillin Hills along Glen Brittle, Isle of Skye, Highland – *opposite*

Old Man of Storr, near Portree, Isle of Skye, Highland

Loch Harport and Glamaig (773m), Isle of Skye, Highland

Dunrobin Castle, near Golspie, Sutherland, Highland

Loch Shin and Benmore Assynt (998m), Sutherland, Highland – *opposite*

Sound of Barra, Isle of Barra, Outer Hebrides

Callanish Standing Stones, Callanish, Isle of Lewis, Outer Hebrides

Cliffs at St John's Head and Old Man of Hoy, Isle of Hoy, Orkney

Fishing boats, Kirkwall
Harbour, Orkney

Flaws Pier, Stromness, Orkney

Noup Head, Isle of Westray, Orkney – *opposite*

Lerwick, Shetland

Scalloway Castle, Scalloway, Shetland

Acknowledgements

Photography by *Graeme Wallace*

Designed by *Melvin Creative*

Reprographics by *GWP Graphics*

Printed by *Printer Trento, Italy*

Published by GW Publishing,

PO Box 6091, Thatcham, Berks, RG19 8XZ.

Tel + 44 (0)1635 268080

First Published 2007

© Copyright GW Publishing

Photographs © Copyright Graeme Wallace

ISBN 978 0 9551564 9 6

To order other publications visit www.gwpublishing.com

Glen Tarff looking towards Glen Mor, Inverness-shire, Highland

Front Cover: Dunnottar Castle, Aberdeenshire

Back Cover: Holm Sound, Orkney